THE COUNTRY
HOUSE-WIFE'S GARDEN

Also available in 'Country Classics':

The Gardener's Essential Gertrude Jekyll
The Essential Gilbert White of Selborne
Life in a Devon Village by Henry Williamson
Memoirs of a Surrey Labourer by George Bourne
A Cotswold Village by J. Arthur Gibbs
Sweet Thames Run Softly by Robert Gibbings
Adventures Among Birds by W.H. Hudson

William Lawson's

THE COUNTRY HOUSE-WIFE'S GARDEN

Containing Rules for Herbs and Seeds of common use, with their Times and Seasons when to Set and Sow them

Together with

THE HUSBANDRY OF BEES

Published with Secrets very necessary for every Housewife: As also divers new Knots for Gardens

And Selections from

A NEW ORCHARD AND GARDEN

With an Introduction by Rosemary Verey

Genesis. 2. 29
*I have given unto you every Herb,
and every Tree, that shall be to you for meat.*

LONDON

Breslich & Foss
43 Museum Street
London WC1A 1LY

The Country House-wife's Garden
first published in 1617
Published by Breslich & Foss 1983 from the 3rd Edition
This edition © Breslich & Foss
Introduction © Rosemary Verey
Series design: Lawrence & Gerry Design Group

All rights reserved. No part of this publication
may be reproduced in any form or by any means
without permission of the publishers

British Library Cataloguing
in Publication Data
Lawson, William
   The country housewife's garden.
   1. Gardening – Early works to 1800
   2. Women – Recreation
   I. Title
   635'.024042   SB454
ISBN 1-85004-012-5   Pbk
ISBN 1-85004-007-9   Hbk

Typeset by Rowland Phototypesetting (London) Ltd.
Printed in Great Britain by
Richard Clay (The Chaucer Press) Ltd,
Bungay, Suffolk.

CONTENTS

Introduction   *page* 7

THE COUNTRY HOUSE-WIFE'S GARDEN

Chap. I *The Soyl*	13
II *Of the Sites*	14
III *Of the Form*	15
IV *Of the Quantity*	21
V *Of Fence*	21
VI *Of two Gardens*	22
VII *Divisions of Herbs*	24
VIII *Husbandry of Herbs*	25
IX *General Rules in Gardening*	33
X *The Husbandry of Bees*	35

Selections from A NEW ORCHARD AND GARDEN

Preface	48
Chap. I *Of the Gardener, and his Wages*	49
XI *Of the right dressing of Trees*	51
XIII *Of Annoyances*	53
XV *Of gathering and keeping Fruit*	56
XVII *Ornaments*	58

INTRODUCTION

William Lawson was a true countryman. His two books *The Countrie Housewifes Garden* of 1617 and *The New Orchard and Garden* published the following year, written for the husbands, far outshine in their appeal and earthy knowledge the sixteenth-century books on gardening, based largely on the classical writers, or translated from later French, German and Latin writings.

Everything William Lawson writes comes straight from the heart and from his own experience of life and of gardening; nothing is plagiarized from other writers. He was a skilful horticulturist and a natural teacher who possessed a flair for sharing his country wisdom. Until recently all we knew about him were the facts which emerge from his books. He lived in Yorkshire on the southern shore of the estuary of the River Tees where he furnished his 'Northern Orchard and Country Garden with needful plants and useful herbs.' He had been gardening for forty-eight years before his two books were published, so all he wrote was genuine inspiration from his own working knowledge. A fact not to be overlooked at that time.

John Harvey*, through recent research, has discovered that our author was a clergyman, instituted vicar of Ormsby, one of the two Teesmouth parishes, on 22 April 1583, which living he held until he died aged 81 in 1635. This evidence makes many facets of his writing fall into place; his knowledge of the classics combined with his closeness to nature, and his ability to express his feelings and associate these with his beliefs. 'What was Paradise? but a Garden, an Orchard of Trees and Herbs, full of pleasure, and nothing there but delights . . . What can your eye desire to see, your nose to smell, your mouth to take that is not to be had in an Orchard?'.

*Country Life, 28 October 1982, 'William Lawson and his Orchard'

In his Preface he explains that he had worked all those years in his orchard and garden and that he shows a 'Plain and sure way of planting'. His friends and neighbours came to see him, so he showed them everything; his new grafts, slips and sets and the best form of an orchard. They saw what he had written, but not yet published, about the best methods of propagating and then cultivating the fruit trees. 'They did see and seeing desired it.' And so in 1618 his delightful and scholarly book, *The New Orchard and Garden*, was published. It is full of natural wisdom concerning the gardener, his labour and wages, the best site and soil, about fences and walls, of settes, slippes and signs of disease, of grafting, dressing and harvesting. In fact it contains 'the best, sure and readiest way to make a good orchard and garden.' He does not tell us if he employed a gardener himself, nor does he mention if he had a wife, but with his direct approach he says, 'If you be not able, nor willing to hire a gardener, keep your profits to yourself, but then you must take all the pains.'

However, I believe it is the final chapter telling about the Ornaments of a garden, of the flowers, Rose red, Damask, Velvet, the sweet Musk-Rose, the fair sweet-scenting Woodbine, double cowslips and primroses and a passing mention of herbs which must have inspired the housewives. 'Rosemary and sweet eglantine are seemly ornaments about a Door or Window.' It would have been natural for the wives to visit William Lawson with their husbands and doubtless they were amazed by all they saw, including how he grew herbs for the pot with such success and his achievement in making his garden so beautiful. I can imagine them first entreating him to show them more and then to write it all down – how to grow good carrots and cabbages and herbs of all sorts. When should they plant these and how to save their own seed? They wanted herbs to make medicines for the still-room and others to add to their salads and soups. They wanted this knowledge urgently and asked him to write this before he finished his book about the orchard.

Thus one of the most entrancing books on gardening may have come to be written. It was published the year before *The New Orchard and Garden,* a slim volume, full of practical advice from a kindly and gentle clergyman who had devoted many years of his life to creating a garden both useful and beautiful and a rich orchard of fruit trees. This book fulfilled a need in the lives of his own parishioners and of others all over the country – ladies longing to be good housewives but lacking the necessary knowledge.

Before the Dissolution of the Monasteries country people were able to turn to the monks in their herb gardens for help and treatment when any of their household were ill. However, it was now the responsibility of the housewife, especially in remote country districts where the services of a learned physician or apothecary were costly and hard to come by. They spent much time in the still-room and several books had already been written for them on the subject of still-room receipts and delights.

It was necessary for the lady of the house to have many talents and qualities; she should be able to read, for it is unlikely that any of her maids could do so. She must be able to instruct them in the art of making all kinds of comfits, confections, sweet-bags and syrups.

A ready supply of medicines, dried herbs and mixed potions must be kept prepared for emergencies; cut fingers, headaches and the hundred-and-one daily occurrences in a large and bustling houshold. As well as all this our good housewife would want fresh vegetables and herbs to help vary and flavour the meals she provided, especially in winter-time when meat and fish were in short supply. 'Gather for the pot and medicines, herbs tender and green, the sap being in the top, but in winter the root is best.' . . . 'A good House-wife may, and will gather store of herbs for the pot, about Lammas, and dry them, and pound them, and in winter they will do good service.' Timely advice.

The ladies were surely delighted with their short book, simply and clearly written. Wise William Lawson does not try to teach them too much all at once. He instructs them how to grow about fifty different herbs, vegetables and flowers commenting 'I reckon these herbs only, because I teach my country housewife, not skilled artists . . . Let her first grow cunning in this, and then she may enlarge her Garden as her skill and ability increaseth.'

The kindly old man explains that they should have two gardens, one for flowers and a kitchen garden, but the distinction need not be too severe. The flower garden may have herbs growing in the 'Squares and knots' and the vegetable garden could have a comely border with abundance of roses and lavender, for those 'yield much profit and comfort to the senses.' The kitchen garden can never look so perfect in form as it 'must yield daily Roots or other Herbs, and suffer deformity.' In fact when a few of the cabbages are cut the prettiness of the row is spoilt.

He suggests to the houswife that she considers the height of her herbs when she is planting them, and place the tallest, such as hollyhocks, lilies, fennel and lovage by walls or in the borders. The lowest must be grown in the front. This is perhaps one of the earliest written suggestions about planting a border in a thought-out, artistic manner. However, always practical, it is important to have the beds divided, that you may go betwixt to weed. His General Rules for Gardening contain sound wisdom, one of the most charming being his advice to have banks and seats of camomile, Penny-royal, Daisies and Violets for these are 'seemly and comfortable.' We should all have plenty of time to sit in our gardens!

Part of William Lawson's great appeal is the natural manner in which he mixes practical advice with his own feelings and artistic discoveries. Writing of weeding, 'I advise the Mistress either to be present herself, or to teach her maids to know herbs from weeds.' We all know the misery of our most treasured plant being weeded away by the jobbing gardener, but as well we must pause and appreciate the magic of our garden for 'Whereas every other pleasure commonly fills some one of our senses, this makes all our senses swim in pleasure, and that with infinite variety.'

As for the Bees, these must be an important, in fact an essential part of the garden. He is emphatic, almost severe about this. 'I will not account her any of my good House-wives, that wanteth either Bees, or skilfulness about them.' He was a Bee-master himself and knew from experience that bees, well ordered, make as much for ornament in the garden as either flowers or form. Perhaps he was not aware of the vital part played by his bees in the fertilisation of his fruit trees, but he knew about the honey they gave him and how he should hive them, keep them warm in winter and prevent all annoyances such as snails and mice from coming to their hives.

The good house-wife should love her bees, and if she followed his advice written in this book she would be as successful in her bee-keeping as she would be in her new-found joy in her garden.

It is easy to picture our clergyman gardener walking round his garden, down by the river, with a group of his parishioners and their families, all delighting in the June scents and promise of a rich harvest. He would have given them sprigs of sage and thyme and a basket of ripe gooseberries. Maybe it was too late that year for them to plant many of the herbs and trees they were enjoying, but by Michaelmas they should have prepared their ground, taken slips and sets and gathered ripe seeds for next year's sowing. To do this the housewives must understand how and when it should all be done. Here was their fount of knowledge. He must not only tell them and show them what to do, but he must write it all down so they will not forget. They wished their gardens to be as productive and alluring as his.

Rosemary Verey, 1983

The Publishers would like to acknowledge gratefully Rosemary Verey's help in the preparation of this edition.

CHAP. I.

The Soyl.

THE Soyl of an Orchard and Garden differ only in these three points : First, the Gardens soil would be somewhat dryer, becuase herbs being more tender then trees, can neither abide moisture nor drought, in such excessive measures as trees ; and therefore having a drier soyl, the remedy is easie against drought : if need be, water soundly, which may be done with small labour, the compass of a Garden being nothing so great as of an Orchard : and this is the cause (if they know it) that Gardeners raise their squares ; but if moisture trouble you, I see no remedy without a general danger, except in Hops, which delight much in a low and sappy earth.   Hops.

    Secondly, the soyl of a Garden would be plain and level, at least every square, (for we purpose the square to be the fittest form) the reason is, the herbs of a garden wanting such helps as should stay the water, which an orchard hath, & the roots of herbs being mellow and loose, is soon either washt away, or sends out his heart by too much drenching and washing.

(marginal notes: Dry. Hops.)

Thirdly, if a Garden soil be not clear of weeds, and namely of graft, the herbs shall never thrive ; for how should good herbs prosper, when evil weeds wax so fast, considering good herbs are tender in respect of evil weeds : these being strengthened by nature, and the other by art? Gardens have small place in comparison, and therefore may more easily be followed, at the least one half year before, and the better dressed after it is framed. And you shall find that clean keeping doth not onely avoid danger of gathering weeds, but also is a special ornament, and leaves more plentifully sap for your tender herbs.

CHAP. II.

Of the Sites.

I Cannot see in any sort, how the site of the one should not be good and fit for the other : The ends of both being one, good, wholesome, and much fruit joyned with delight, unless trees be more able to abide the nipping frosts than tender herbs ; but I am sure, the flowers of trees are as soon perished with cold, as any herb, except Pumpion and Melons.

CHAP. III.

Of the Form.

Let that which is said in the Orchards form, suffice for a Garden in general : but for special forms in squares, they are as many, as there are devices in Gardiners brains. Neither is the wit and art of a skilful Gardiner in this point not to be commended, that can work more variety for breeding of more delightsome choice, and of all those things where the owner is able and desirous to be satisfied. The number of Forms, Mazes, and Knots is so great, and men are so diversly delighted, that I leave every House-wife to her self, especially seeing to set down many, had been but to fill much paper ; yet lest I deprive her of all delight and direction, let her view these few, choice, new forms ; and note this generally, that all plots are square, and all are bordered about with Privit, Raisins, Fea-berries, Roses, Thorn, Rosemary, Bee-flowers, Hysop, Sage, or such like.

The ground plot for knots.

Cinkfoil.

Flower-de-luce.

The Tre-foy.

The fret.

Lozenge.

Cross-bow.

Diamond.

Oval.

Maze.

CHAP. IV.

Of the Quantity.

A Garden requireth not so large a scope of ground as an Orchard, both in regard of the much weeding, dressing, and removing, and also the pains in a Garden is not so well repayed home, as in an Orchard. It is to be granted, that the Kitchin garden doth yield rich gains, by Berries, Roots, Cabbages, &c. yet these are no way comparable to the fruit of a Rich Orchard : but notwithstanding I am of opinion, that it were better for *England* that we had more Orchards and Gardens, and more large. And therefore, we leave the quantity to every man's ability and will.

CHAP. V.

Of Fence.

SEeing we allow Gardens in Orchard plots, and the benefit of a Garden is much, they both require a strong and shrowding fence. Therefore leaving this, let us come to the Herbs themselves, which must be the fruit of all these labours.

CHAP. VI.

Of two Gardens.

HErbs are of two sorts, and therefore it is meet, (they requiring divers manners of Husbandry) that we have two Gardens ; a garden for flowers, and a Kitchin garden ; or a Summer garden : not that we mean so perfect a distinction, that we mean the Garden for flowers should or can be without herbs good for the Kitchin, or the Kitchin-garden should want flowers, nor on the contrary ; but for the most part they would be severed : first, because your Garden-flowers shall suffer some disgrace, if among them you intermingle Onions, Parsnips, &c. Secondly, your Garden that is durable, must be of one form : but that which is your Kitchins use, must yield daily Roots, or other herbs, and suffer deformity. Thirdly, the herbs of both will not be both alike ready, at one time, either for gathering, or removing. First therefore,

Of the Summer Garden.

THese herbs and flowers are comely and durable for squares & Knots, & all to be set at *Michael-tide*, or somewhat before ; that they may be setled in, and taken with the ground before winter, though they may be Set, especially sown, in the spring.

Roses and all sorts, (spoken of in the Orchard) must be Set. Some use to set slips and twine them, which sometimes, but seldome thrive all.

Rosemary, Lavender, Bee-flowers, Isop, Sage, Time, Cowslips, Piony, Daises, Clove-Gilli-flowers, Pinks, Southernwood, Lillies, of all which hereafter.

Of the Kitchin Garden.

Though your Garden for flowers doth in a sort peculiarly challenge to it self a perfect, and exquisite form to the eyes, yet you may not altogether neglect this, where your herbs for the pot do grow : And therefore some here make comely borders with the herbs aforesaid ; the rather, because abundance of Roses and Lavender, yield much profit, and comfort to the senses : Rosewater, Lavender, the one cordial (as also the Violets, Burrage, and Bugloss) the other reviving the spirits by the sense of smelling, both most durable for smell, both in flowers and water : you need not here raise your beds, as in the other Garden, because Summer towards, will not let too much wet annoy you, and these herbs require more moisture : yet must you have your beds divided, that you may go betwixt to weed, and somewhat of form would be expected : To which it availeth that you place your herbs of biggest growth, by walls, or in borders, as Fennel, &c. and the lowest in the middest, as Saffron, Strawberries, Onions, &c.

CHAP. VII.

Divisions of Herbs.

Garden herbs are innumerable, yet these are common, and sufficient for our Country-house-wives.

Herbs of great growth.

Fennel, Angelica, Tansie, Hollihock, Lovage, Elicampane, French Mallows, Lillies, French Poppy, Endive, Succory and Clary.

Herbs of middle growth.

Burrage, Bugloss, Parsly, Sweet Sicily, Flower-deluce, Stock-Gilli-flowers, Wall-flowers, Anni-seeds, Coriander, Fether-few, Mary-golds, Oculus Christi, Langdibeef, Alexanders, Carduus-Benedictus.

Herbs of smaller growth.

Pansie, or Hearts ease, Coast-Marjoram, Savory, Strawberries, Saffron, Licoras, Daffadowndillies, Leeks, Chives, Chibbals, Skerots, Onions, Bachelors buttons, Daisies, Penny-royal.

Hitherto, I have only reckoned up, and put in this rank, some Herbs: their Husbandry follows, each in an Alphabetical order, the better to be found.

CHAP. VIII

Husbandry of Herbs.

Alexanders, are to be renewed as Angelica. It is a timely Pot-herb.

Angelica is renewed with the seed, whereof he beareth plenty the second year, and so dyeth. You may remove the roots the first year. The leaves distilled, yield water, soveraign to expel pain from the stomach. The Root dried, taken in the fall, stoppeth the pores against infection.

Anniseeds make their growth, and bear seeds the first year, and dieth as Coriander : it is good for opening the pipes, and it is used in Comfits.

Artichoaks, are renewed by dividing the Roots into Sets, in *March*, every third or fourth year. They require a several usuage, and therefore a several whole plot by themselves, especially, considering they are plentiful of fruit much desired.

Burrage, and Bugloss, two Cordials, renew themselves by seed yearly, which is hard to be gathered, they are exceeding good Pot-herbs, good for Bees, and most comfortable for the heart and stomack, as Quinces and Wardens.

Camomile, set roots in banks and walks, it is sweet smelling, qualifying head-ach.

Cabbages, require great room, they seed the second year, sowe them in *February*, remove them when the plants are an handful long, set deep and wet. Look well in drought for the white Caterpillars worm, the spawns under the leaf closely ; for every living Creature doth seek food and quiet shelter, and growing quick they draw to, and eat the heart : you may find them in a rainy dewy morning.

It is a good Pot-herb, and of this herb called *Cole*, our Country-house-wifes give their Pottage their name, and call them *Caell*.

Carduus Benedictus, or blessed Thistle, seeds and dies the first year : the excellent vertue thereof, I refer to Herbals, for we are Gardiners, not Physitians.

Carrets are sown late in *April* or *May*, as Turneps, else they seed the first year, and then their roots are naught : the second year they die, their root grow great, and require large room.

Chibals or Chives, have their roots parted, as Garlick, Lillies, &c. and so are they set every third or fourth year : a good pot-herb, opening, but evil for the eyes.

Clary, is sown, it seeds the second year, and dies. It is somewhat harsh in taste, a little in pottage is good, it strengtheneth the reins.

Coast, Root parted, makes Sets in *March*, it bears the second year ;—it is used in Ale in *May*.

Coriander, is for usage and uses, much like Anniseeds.

Daffadowndillies, have their roots parted, and set once in three or four years, or longer time. They flower timely, and after *Midsummer* are scarcely seen. They are more for Ornament than for use, so are Daisies.

Daisie roots parted and Set, as Flower-deluce, and Camomile, when you see them grow too thick or decay. They be good to keep up, and strengthen the edges of your borders, as Pinks, they be red, white, mixt.

Elicampane-Root is long-lasting, as is the Lovage : it seeds yearly, you may divide the Root, and Set ; the Root taken in Winter is good (being dried, powdered, and drunk) to kill itches.

Endive and Succory, are much like in nature, shape and use, they renew themselves by seed, as Fennel, and other herbs. You may remove them before they put forth shanks : a good Pot-herb.

Fennel is renewed, either by the seeds (which it beareth the second year, and so yearly in great abundance) sown in the fall or Spring, or by dividing one Root into many sets, as Artichoake. It is long of growth and life. You may remove the root unshankt : It is exceeding good for the eyes, distilled, or any otherwise taken : it is used in dressing Hives for swarms, a very good Pot-herb, or for Sallets.

Fether-few shakes seed. Good against a shaking Fever, taken in a posset drink fasting.

Flower-de-luce, long lasting, divide his roots and Set : the roots dryed have a sweet smell.

Garlick may be set an handful distance, two inches deep, in the edge of your beds. Part the heads into several cloves, and every clove set in the latter end of *February*, will increase to a great head before *September* : good for opening, evil for eyes ; when the blade is long, fasten two and two together and the heads will be bigger.

Hollihock riseth high, seedeth and dyeth ; the chief use I know, is ornament.

Isop is reasonable long lasting : young Roots are good Sets, slips better. A good pot-herb.

July-flowers, commonly called Gilly-flowers, or Clove July-flowers, (I call them so, because they flower in *July*) they have the name of Cloves, of their sent. I may well call them the King of flowers except the Rose, & the best sort of them are called Queen-July-flowers. I have of them nine or ten several colours, & divers of them as big as Roses ; of all flowers (save the Damask Rose) they are the most pleasant to sight and smell, they last not past three or four years unremoved. Take the slips (without shanks) and Set any time save in extream frost, but especially at *Michaeltide.* Their use is much in ornament, and comforting the spirits, by the sense of smelling.

July-flowers of the Wall, or Wall July-flowers, Wall-flowers, or Bee-flowers, or Winter-July-flowers, because growing in the walls even in winter, and good for Bees, will grow even in stone-walls, they will seem dead in Summer and yet revive in Winter they yield seed plentifully, which you may sow at any time, or in any broken earth, especially on the top of a mud-wall, but moist ; you may set the root before it be brancht, every slip that is not flowr'd will take root, or crop him in the Summer, and he will flower in Winter, but his Winter seed is untimely. This and Palmes are exceeding good, and timely for Bees.

Leeks yield seed the second year, unremoved, and dye, unless you remove them, usually to eat with Salt and Bread, as Onions always green, good pot-herb, evil for the eyes.

Lavender-spike would be removed within seven years, or eight at the most : slips twined, as Hysop and Sage, would take best at *Michael-tide*. This flower is good for Bees, most comfortable for swelling, except Roses : and kept dry, is as strong after a year, as when it is gathered. The water of this is comfortable.

White *Lavender* would be removed sooner.

Lettice yields seed the first year, and dyes : some betime, and if you would have them Cabbage for sellets, remove them as you do Cabbage. they are usual in Sallets and in the pot.

Lillies white and red, remove once in three or four years, their roots yield many Sets, like the Garlick. *Michael-tide* is the best. They grow high, after they get root. These roots are good to break a boil, as are Mallows and Sorrel.

Mallows, French or gagged, the first or second year, seed plentifully. Sow in *March*, or before. They are good for the housewifes pot, or to break a bunch.

Marigolds, most commonly come of seed, you may remove the Plants when they are two inches long. The double Marigold, being as big as a little Rose, is good for shew. They are a good Pot-herb.

Oculus Christi, or Christs-eye, seeds, and dyes the first or second year : you may remove the young Plants, but seed is better. One of these seeds put into the eye, within three or four hours will gather a thick skin, clear the eye, and bolt it self forth without hurt to the eye. A good Pot-herb.

Onions are sown in *February*, they are gathered at *Michael-tide*, and all the Summer long, for Sallet; as also young Parsly, Sage, Chibals, Lettice, sweet Sicily, Fennel, *&c.* good alone, or with meat, muttons, *&c.* for sawce, especially for the pot.

Parsly sowe the first year, and use the next year : it seeds plentifully, an herb of much use, as sweet Sicily is. The Seed and Roots are good against the stone.

Parsnips require an whole plot, they be plentiful and common, sowe them in *February*, the King's (that is in the middle) seed broadest and reddest. Parsnips are sustenance for a strong stomach, not good for evil eyes : When they cover the earth, in a drought to tread the tops, makes the Roots bigger.

Penny-royal, or pudding-grass, creeps along the ground, like ground Ivy. It lasts long, like daisies, because it puts and spreads daily new roots. Divide, and remove the roots, it hath a pleasant taste & smell, good for the pot, or hackt-meat, or Haggas pudding.

Pumpions, set Seeds with your finger, a finger deep, late in *March*, as so soon as they appear, every night if you doubt frost, cover them, and water them continually out of a water-pot : they be very tender, their fruit is great and waterish.

French-Poppy beareth a great flower, and the seed will make you sleep.

Raddish is sawce for cloyed stomachs, as Capers, Olives, and Cucumbers, cast their seeds all summer long here and there, and you shall have them always young and fresh.

Rosemary, the Grace of Herbs here in *England*, in other Countries common. To set slips immediately after *Lammas*, is the surest way. Seed sown may prove well, so they be sown in hot weather, somewhat moist, and good earth : for the herb, though great, is nesh and tender (as I take it) brought from hot Countries to us in the cold North : set thin, it becomes a window well. The use is much in meats, more in Physick, most for Bees.

Rue, or *Herb of Grace*, continually green, the slips are set. It lasts long, as Rosemary, Southernwood, *&c.* too strong for mine House-wifes pot, unless she will brew Ale therewith, against the Plague : let them not seed if you will have them last.

Saffron, every third year his roots would be removed at *Midsummer*, for when all other Herbs grow most, it dieth. It flowereth at *Michael-tide*, and groweth all Winter : keeps his flowers from Birds in the morning, and gather the yellow, (for they shape much like Lillies) dry, and after dry them, they be precious, expelling diseases from the heart and stomack.

Savory, seeds and dyes the first year, good for my House-wifes pot and pye.

Sage, set slips in *May*, and they grow aye ; let it not seed, it will last the longer. The use is much and common. The Monkish Proverb is *tritum*.

Cur moreatur homo, cui salvia crescit in horto?

Skerots, the Roots are set when they are parted, as *Plony*, and Flower-deluce at *Michael-tide*, the Root is but small and very sweet, I know none other special use but the Table.

Sweet *Sicily*, long lasting, pleasantly tasting, either the seed is sown, or the root parted, or removed, makes increase, it is of like use with Parsley.

Strawberries, long lasting, set Roots at *Michaeltide*, or the Spring, they be red, white and green, and ripe, when they be great and soft, some by *Midsummer* with us. The use is, they will cool my Housewife well, if they be put in Wine or Cream with Sugar.

Time, both seeds, slips, and Roots are good, if it seed not, it will last three or four years or more, it smelleth comfortably. It hath much use, namely, in all cold meats, it is good for Bees.

Turnip, is sown : In the second year they bear plenty of seed ; they require the same time of sowing that Carrets do : they are sick of the same disease that Cabbages be. The root increaseth much, it is most wholesome, if it be sown in a good and well tempered earth ; Soveraign for eyes and bees.

I reckon these herbs only, because I teach my Country Housewife, not skilful Artists ; and it should be an endless labour, and would make the matter tedious to reckon up *Land-chief, Stock-Gillyflowers, Charvel, Valerian, Go to bed at noon, Piony, Lidoras, Tansie, Garden-Mints, Germander, Centaury,* and a thousand such Physick Herbs. Let her first grow cunning in this, and then she may inlarge her Garden as her skill and ability encreaseth. And to help her the more, I have set down these Observations.

CHAP. IX.

General Rules in Gardening.

IN the South parts Gardening may be more timely, and more safely done then with us in *Yorkshire*, because our air is not so favourable, nor our ground so good.

2. Secondly, most seeds shake, by turning the good earth, are renewed, their Mother the earth keeping them in her bowels, till the Sun their Father can reach them with his heat.

3. In setting herbs, leave no top more than a handful above the ground, nor more than a foot under the earth.

4. Twine the roots of those slips you set, if they will abide it. Gilly-flowers are too tender.

5. Set moist, and sow dry.

6. Set slips without shanks at any time, except at *Midsummer*, and in frosts.

7. Seeding spoils the most roots, as drawing the heart and sap from the root.

8. Gather for the pot and medicines, herbs tender and green, the sap being in the top, but in Winter the root is best.

9. All the herbs in the Garden for flowers would once in seven years be renewed, or soundly watered with puddle water, except Rosemary.

10. In all your Gardens and Orchards, Banks and Seats of Camomile, Penny-royal, Daisies and Violets, are seemly and comfortable.

11. These require whole plots: Artichoaks, Cabbages, Turnips, Parsnips, Onions, Carrets, and (if you will) Saffron and Skerrits.

12. Gather all your seeds, dead, ripe and dry.

13. Lay not dung to the roots of your herbs, as usually they do: for dung not melted is too hot even for Trees.

14. Thin setting and sowing (so the roots stand not past a foot distance) is profitable, for the herbs will like the better. Greater herbs would have more distance.

15. Set and sow herbs in their time of growth, (except at *Midsummer* for then they are too tender) but Trees in their time to rest.

16. A good House-wife may, and will gather store of herbs for the pot, about Lammas, and dry them, and pound them, and in winter they will do good service.

Thus I have lined out a Garden to our Country House-wives, and given them Rules for common herbs. If any of them (as sometimes they are) be knotty, I refer them to Chap. 3. The skill and pains of weeding the Garden with weeding knives of fingers, I refer to themselves, and their maids, willing them to take the opportunity of a shower of rain; withal, I advise the Mistress either to be present her self, or to teach her maids to know herbs from weeds.

CHAP. X.

The Husbandry of Bees.

THere remaineth one necessary thing to be prescribed, which in mine Opinion makes as much for Ornament, as either flowers, or form, or cleanness, and I am sure as commodious as any of, or all the rest : which is Bees, well ordered. And I will not account her any of my good House-wives, that wanteth either Bees, or skilfulness about them. And though I know some have written well and truly, and others more plentifully upon this Theme : yet somewhat have I learned by experience, (being a Bee-master my self) which hitherto I cannot find put into writing, for which I think our House-wives will count themselves beholding unto me.

The first thing that a Gardiner about Bees must be careful for, is, an house, not stakes and stones abroad, *Sub dio* : for stakes rot and reel, Rain and Weather eat your hivers and covers, and cold most of all is hurtful for your Bees. Therefore you must have an house made along a sure dry wall in your Garden, near or in your Orchard : For Bees love flowers and wood with their hearts.

Bee-houses.

This the form ; a Frame standing on posts with one floor (if you would have it hold more Hives, two floors) boarded, laid on bearers, and back posts, covered over with boards, flat-wise.

Let the floors be without holes or clifts, lest in

casting time the Bees lie out and loyter.

And though your Hives stand within an hand-breadth the one of another, yet will the Bees know their home.

In this Frame may your Bees stand dry and warm, especially if you make doors, like doors of windows, to shroud them in winter, as an house : provided you leave the hives mouth open. I my self have devised such an house, and I find that it strengthens my Bees much, and my Hives will last six to one.

Hives.

Mr. *Markham* commends Hives of Wood : I discommend them not : but straw hives are in use with us, and I think, with all the World, which I commend for nimbleness, closeness, warmness and driness. Bees love no external motions of daubing,

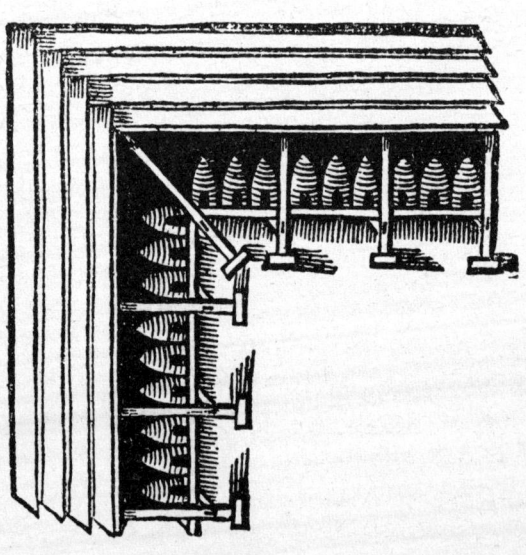

or such like. Sometimes occasion shall be offered to lift and turn hives, as shall appear hereafter. One light entire hive of straw, in that case, is better than one that is daubed, weighty and cumbersome. I wish every hive, for a keeping swarm, to hold three pecks at least by measure ; for too little hives procure Bees, in casting time, either to lie out and loyter, or else to cast before they be ripe and strong, and so make weak swarms and untimely : whereas if they have room sufficient they ripen timely, and casting seasonably, are strong, & fit for labour presently. Neither would the Hive be too great, for then they loyter, and waste meat and time.

Your Bees delight in wood, for feeding, especially for casting, therefore want not an Orchard. A *May's* swarm is worth a Mares Foal : if they want wood, they be in danger of flying away. Any time before *Midsummer* is good for casting, and timely ; before *July* is not evil. I much like Mr. *Markham's* opinion, for having a swarm in combs of a dead or forsaken hive, so they be fresh and cleanly. To think that a swarm of your own, or others, will of it self come into any such hive, is a meer conceit, *Experto crede Roberto*. His smearing with honey is to no purpose, for the other Bees will eat it up. If your swarm knit in the top of a tree, as they will, if the wind beat them not to fall down, let the stool or ladder prescribed in the Orchard do you service. *[Hiving of Bees.]*

The less the Spelks are, the less is the waste of your honey, & the more easily will they draw, when you take your Bees. Four Spelks athwart, and one top Spelk are sufficient. The Bees will fasten their combs *[Spelks.]*

to the hive. A little honey is good, but if you want, Fennel will serve to rub your hive withal. The Hive being drest, and ready spelkt, rub'd, and the hole made for their passage, (I use no hole in the Hive, but a piece of wood hoal'd, to save the Hive, & keep out mice) shake in your Bees, or the most of them (for all commonly you cannot get) the remainder will follow. Many use smoak, nettles, &c. which I entirely dislike; for Bees love not to be molested. Ringing in the time of casting is a meer fancie: violent handling of them is simply evil, because Bees of all other creatures love cleanliness, and peace. Therefore handle them leisurely, and quietly, and their Keeper, whom they know, may do with them what he will without hurt: Being hived at night, bring them to their seat. Set your Hives all of one year together.

Signes of breeding, if they be strong.

1. They will avoid dead young Bees and Drones.
2. They will sweat in the morning, till it run from them, always when they be strong.

Signes of casting.

1. They will fly Droans by reason of heat.
2. The young Swarms will once or twice, in some fair season come forth mustring, as though they would cast, to prove themselves, and go in again.
3. The night before they cast, if you lay your ear to the hives mouth, you shall hear two or three, but

especially one above the rest, cry, Up, up, up, or Tout, tout, tout, like a Trumpet sounding the alarum to the battel.

  Much descanting there is of, and about the Master Bee, and their degrees, order and Government : but the truth in this point is rather imagined, than demonstrated. There are some conjectures of it, *viz.* we see in the combs divers greater houses than the rest, and we commonly hear the night before they cast, sometime one Bee, sometime two or more Bees, give a loud and several sound from the rest, and sometimes Bees of greater bodies than the common sort : But what of all this? I lean not on conjectures, but love to set down what I know to be true, and leave these things to them that love to divine.

  Keep none weak, for it is hazard oftentimes with loss. Feeding will not keep them : for being weak, they cannot come down to meat, if they come down, they die, because weak Bees cannot abide cold. If none of these, yet will the other Bees, being strong, smell the honey, and come, and spoil, and kill them. Some helps is in casting time, to put two weak swarms together, or as Mr. *Markham* well saith, Let them not cast late, by raising them with wood or stone, but with imps (say I.) An imp is, three or four wreaths wrought as the Hive, the same compass to raise the Hive withal ; but by experience in trial, I have found out a better way by Clustering, for late or weak swarms ; hitherto not found out of any that I know. That is this : After casting time, If I have any stock proud, and hindred from timely

_{Catching.}

_{Clustering.}

casting, with former Winters poverty, or evil weather in casting time, with two handles and crooks fitted for the purpose, I turn that stock so pestered with Bees, and set it on the crown, upon which so turned with the mouth upward, I place another empty hive well drest, and spelkt, into which, without any labour, the swarm that would not depart, and cast, will presently ascend, because the old Bees have this quality (as all other breeding creatures have) to expel the young, when they have brought them up.

There will the Swarm build as kindly, as if they had of themselves been cast. But be sure you lay betwixt the Hives some straight and cleanly stick or sticks, or rather a board with holes, to keep them asunder : otherwise they will joyn their works together so fast, that they cannot be parted. If you so keep them asunder at *Michael-tide*, if you like the weight of your swarm (for the goodness of swarms is tried by the weight) so catched, you may set it by for a stock to keep. Take heed in any case the combs be not broken, for then the other Bees will smell the honey, and spoil them. This have I tried to be very profitable for the saving of Bees.

The Instrument hath this form. The great strait

piece of wood the rest are iron clasps & nails, the

clasps are loose in the staple, 2 men with two of these fastned to the Hive, will easily turn it up.

They gather not till *July* ; for then they be discharged of their young, or else they are become now strong to labour ; & now sap in flowers is strong and proud, by reason of time, & force of Sun. And now also in the North (and not before) the herbs of greatest vigour put forth their flowers ; as Beans, Fennel, Burrage, &c.

The most sensible weather for them, is heat and draught, because the nesh Bee can neither abide cold nor wet ; and showers (which they well fore-see) do interrupt their labours, unless they fall in the night, and so they further them.

After casting time, you shall benefit stocks much, if you help them to kill their Droans, which by all probability and judgment, are an idle kind of Bees, and wastful. Some say they breed, and have seen young Droans in taking their honey, which I know is true. But I am of opinion, that there are also Bees which have lost their stings, and so being as it were gelded, become idle and great : there is great use of them. *Deus & Natura nihil fecit frustra.* "They hate the Bees, and cause them cast the sooner; they never come forth, but when they be over-heated ; they never come home loaden." After casting-time, & when the Bees want meat, "You shall see the labouring Bees fasten on them, two, three or four at once, as if they were thieves to be led to the Gallows, and killing them, they cast them out, and draw them far from home, as hateful enemies." Our House-wife, if she be the keeper of her own Bees (as

Droans.

she had need to be) may with her bare hand in the heat of the day safely destroy them in the hives mouth. Some use towards night, in a hot day, to set before the mouth of the hive a thin board with little holes in it, at which the lesser Bees may enter, but not the Droans ; so that you may kill them at your pleasure.

Annoyances. Snails spoil them by night like thieves ; they come so quietly, and are so fast, that the Bees fear them not ; look early and late, especially in a rainy or dewy evening or morning.

Mice are no less hurtful, and the rather to Hives of straw : and therefore coverings of straw draw them : they will in, either at the mouth, or shear themselves an hole : The remedy is good Cats, Rates-bane and watching.

The cleanly Bee hateth the smoak as poyson : therefore let your Bees stand nearer your Garden, than your Brewhouse or Kitchin. They say Sparrows and Swallows are enemies to Bees ; but I see it not.

More Hives perish by Winters cold, than by all other hurts ; for the Bee is tender and nice, and only lives in warm weather, and dies in cold. And therefore, let my House-wife be perswaded, that a warm dry house before described, is the chiefest help she can make her Bees against this, and many more mischiefs. Many use against cold in Winter, to stop up their hive close ; & some set them in houses, persuading themselves, that thereby they relieve their Bees. First, tossing, moving is hurtful. Secondly, in houses, going, knocking and shaking is noisome. Thirdly too much heat in an house is unnatural for them. But lastly, & especially, Bees cannot abide to be stopt up close ; for at every warm season of the Sun they revive, & living eat, and eating must needs purge abroad : in her house the cleanly Bee will not purge her self. Judge you what it is for any living creature, not to disburthen nature. Being shut up in calm seasons, lay your ear to the Hive, and you shall hear them yearn and yell, as so many hundred prisoners. Therefore impound not your Bee, so profitable and free a Creature.

 Let none stand above three years, else the combs will be black and knotty, your honey will be thin and uncleanly ; and if any cast after three years, it is such as have swarms of old Bees, kept all together, which is great loss. Smoking with Rags, Rozen or Brimstone, many use ; some use drowning in a tub of clean water, and the water well brew'd will be a good botchet. Draw out your spelks immediately with a pair of pinchers, lest the Wood grow soft and swell, and so will not be drawn, then must you cut your hive. Taking of Bees.

 Let no fire come near your Honey, for fire softneth the wax and dross, and makes them run with the honey : Fire softneth, weakneth, and hindreth honey from purging. Break your combs small, when the dead empty combs are parted from the loaden combs into a sieve, born over a great bowl or vessel with two staves, and so let it run two or three days : the sooner you run it up, the better will it purge. Run your swarm honey by it self, and that shall be your best. The elder your Hives are, the Straining Honey.

worse is your honey.

Vessels.

Usual Vessels are of Clay, but after wood be satiated with Honey (for it will leak at first; for honey is marvellously searching, though thick, and therefore virtuous) I use it rather, because it will not break so soon with falls, frosts, or otherwise, and greater Vessels of clay will hardly last.

When you use your Honey, with a spoon take off the skin, which it hath put up.

And it is worth the regard, that Bees thus used, if you have but forty stocks, shall yield you more commodity clearly than forty Acres of Ground.

And thus much may suffice, to make good House-wifes love, and have good Gardens and Bees.

DEO LAUS.

Selections from

A NEW ORCHARD & GARDEN

OR

The best way for Planting, Graffing, and to make any Ground good for a Rich Orchard : Particularly in the North, and Generally for the whole Common-wealth, as in Nature, Reason, Situation, and all Probability, may and doth appear.

THE PREFACE

To all Well-minded.

... Whereupon have I, of my meer and sole Experience, without respect to any former written Treatise, gathered these Rules, and set them down in writing, not daring to hide the least Talent given me of my Lord and Master in Heaven. Neither is this injurious to any, though it differ from the Common opinion in divers points, to make it known to others, what good I have found out, in this faculty by long tryal and experience. I confess freely my want of Curious Skill in the Art of Planting : and I admire and praise Pliny, Aristotle, Virgil, Cicero, and many others, for wit and judgment in this kind, and leave them to their times, manner, and several countries ...

And I shew a plain and sure way of Planting, which I have found good by 48 Years (and more) experience in the North part of England. I prejudicate and envy none ; wishing yet all to abstain from maligning that good (to them unknown) which is well intended. Farewell.

Thine for thy good,

W. L.

CHAP. I.

Of the Gardener, and his Wages.

Whosoever desireth and endeavoureth to have a Pleasant and Profitable *Orchard*, must (if he be able) provide himself of a Fruiterer, Religious, Honest, Skilful in that Faculty, and therewithal Painful . . . *Religious.*

Honesty in a Gardener, will grace your Garden, and all your house, and help to stay unbridled Serving-men, giving offence to none, not calling your Name into Question by dishonest acts, nor infecting your Family by evil counsel or example. For there is no Plague so infectious as Popery and Knavery ; he will not purloin your profit, nor hinder your pleasures . . . *Honest.*

The *Gardener* had not need be an idle or lazy Lubber, forso your *Orchard*, being a matter of such moment, will not prosper, there will ever be something to do. Weeds are always growing, the great Mother of all living Creatures, the Earth, is full of feed in her Bowels, and any stirring gives them heat of Sun, and being laid near day, they grow : Moles work daily, though not always alike : Winter Herbs at all times will grow (except in extream Frost.) In Winter your Trees and Herbs would be lightned of Snow, and your Allies cleansed : drifts of Snow will set Deer, Hares and Conies, and other noysome Beasts, over your Walls *Painful.*

and Hedges in your *Orchard*. When Summer cloath your Borders with Green and speckled colours, your *Gardener* must dress his Hedges, and antick works ; watch his Bees, and hive them : distill his Roses and other Herbs. Now begin Summer Fruits to ripen, and crave your hand to pull them. If he have a *Garden* (as he must needs) to keep, you must needs allow him good help, to end his labours which are endless ; for no one man is sufficient for these things.

<small>Wages.</small>

Such a *Gardener* as will conscionably, quietly and patiently travel in your *Orchard*, God shall Crown the labours of his hands with joyfulness, and make the Clouds drop fatness upon your Trees ; he will provoke your love, and earn his wages and fees belonging to his place. The house being served, fallen fruit, superfluity of Herbs and Flowers, Seed, Graffs, Sets, and besides all other of that Fruit which your bountiful hand shall reward him withal, will much augment his wages, and the profit of your Bees will pay you back again.

If you be not able, nor willing to hire a *Gardener*, keep your profits to your self, but then you must take all the pains ; and for that purpose (if you want this faculty) to instruct you, have I undertaken these Labours, and gathered these Rules, but chiefly respecting my Countries good.

CHAP. XI.

Of the right dressing of Trees.

IF all these things aforesaid were indeed performed, as we have shew'd them in words, you should have a perfect Orchard, nature and substance, begun to your hand : and yet are all these things nothing, if you want that skill to keep and dress your Trees. Such is the condition of all earthly things, whereby a man receiveth profit, or pleasure, that they degenerate presently without good ordering. Man himself, left to himself, grows from his heavenly and spiritual generation, and becometh beastly, yea, devilish to his own kind, unless he be regenerate. No marvel then, if Trees make their shoots, and put their sprays disorderly. And truly (if I were worthy to judge) there is not a mischief that breedeth greater and more general harm to all the Orchard, (especially, if they be any continuance) that ever I saw, (I will not except three) than the want of the skilful dressing of trees. It is a common, and unskilful opinion, and saying, Let all grow, and they will bear more fruit : and if thou lop away superfluous boughs, they say, what a pity is this ? how many Apples would these have born? not considering, there may arise hurt to your Orchard . . .

This is the best form of a fruit-tree, which I have here shaddowed out for the better capacity of them that are led more with the eye, then the mind, craving pardon for the deformity, because I am

<small>Necessity of dressing trees.</small>

<small>General rule.</small>

nothing skilful either in the painting or carving.

Imagine that the paper makes but one side of the tree to appear, the whole round compass will give leave for many more arms, boughs, branches, and cyons.

The perfect form of a Fruit-Tree.

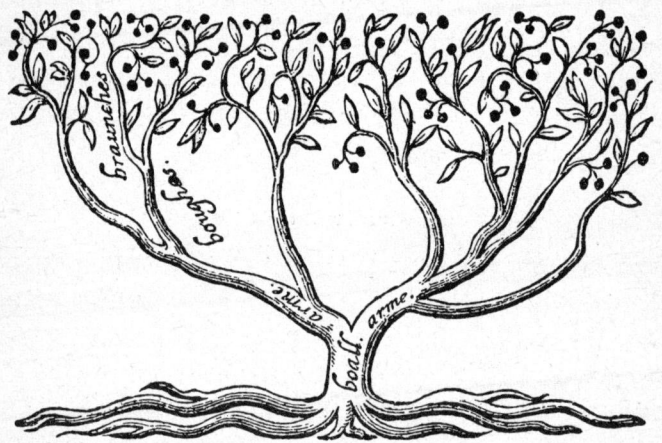

If any tree cannot well be brought to this form : *Experto crede Roberto*, I can shew divers of them under twenty years of age.

The fittest time of the Moon for proyning, is, as of grafting, when the sap is ready to stir (not proudly stirring) and so to cover the wound : and of the year, a month before (or at least when) you graff. Dress Pears, Apricocks, Peaches, Cherries, and Bullis sooner. And old trees before young plants, you may dress at any time betwixt Leaf and Leaf. And note, where you take any thing away, the sap the next Summer will be putting : Be sure therefore when he puts a bud in any place where you would not have him, rub it off with your finger . . .

CHAP. XIII.

Of Annoyances.

... See you here an whole Army of mischiefs banded in troops against the most fruitful trees the earth bears? assailing your labours. Good things have most enemies.

A skilful Fruiterer must put to his helping hand, and disband and put them to flight. *Remedy.*

For the first rank of beasts, besides your out-strong fence, you must have a fair and swift Grey-hound, a Stonebow, Gun, and if need require, an Apple with an hook for a Deer, and an Hare-pipe for an Hare. *Deer, &c.*

Your Cherries, and other Berries, when they be ripe, will draw all the Black-birds, Thrushes, and Mag-pies, to your Orchard. The Bul-finch is a devourer of your fruit in the bud, I have had whole Trees shall'd out with them in Winter-time. *Birds.*

The best remedy here is a Stone-bow, a Piece, especially if you have a musket, or sparrow-hawk in winter, to make the Black-bird stoop into a bush, or hedge.

The Gardner must cleanse his soil of all other trees, but fruit-trees, as aforesaid, *chap.* 2. for which it is ordained ; and I would especially name Oaks, Elms, Ashes, and such other great wood, but that I doubt it would be taken as an admission of lesser trees ; for I admit of nothing to grow in my Orchard but fruit and flowers : if sap can hardly be good to feed our fruit-trees, should we allow of any other?

especially those that will become their Masters, and wrong them in their lively-hood?

Winds.

And though we admit without the fence, of wall-nuts in most plain places, Trees middle-most and Ashes, or Oaks, or Elms utmost, set in comely rows equally distant, with fair Allies twixt row and row, to avoid the boisterous blasts of winds, and within them also others for bees, yet we admit none of these into your Orchard plat : other remedies then this have we none against the nipping frost.

Frosts.
Weeds.

Weeds in fertile soil, (because the general course is so) till your trees grow great, will be noisome, and deform your allies, walks, beds, and squares ; your under gardeners must labour to keep all cleanly, and handsome from them, and all other filth, with a spade, weeding knives, rake with Iron teeth, a scraple of Iron thus formed.

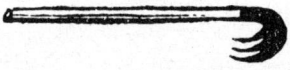

For Nettles, and ground Ivy after a showr.

When weeds, straw, sticks, and all other scrapings are gathered together, burn them not, but bury them under your crust in any place of your Orchard, and they will dye, and fatten your ground.

Worms.
Moals.

Worms and Moals open the earth, and let in air to the Roots of your trees, and deform your squares and walks ; and feeding in the earth, being in number infinite, draw on barrenness.

Remedy.

Worms may easily be destroyed. Any Summer evening, when it is dark, after a showr with a candle you may fill bushels ; but you must tread nimbly, and where you cannot come to catch them, so sift the earth with coal-ashes an inch or two thickness, and that is a plague to them, so is sharp gravel.

Moals will anger you if your Gardiner or some other moal-catcher ease you not, especially, having made their fortresses among the Roots of your Trees ; you must watch her well with a Moal-spear, at morning, noon, and night : when you see her utmost hill, cast a trench betwixt he and her home, for she hath a princepal mansion to dwell and breed in about *April*, which you may discern by a principal hill, wherein you may catch her, if you trench it round, and sure, and watch well ; or wheresoever you can discern a single passage, (for such she hath) there trench, and watch, and have her.

Wilful annoyances must be prevented, and avoided by the love of the master, and Fruiterer. which they bear to their Orchard.

Justice and liberality will put away evil neighbours, or evil neighbour-hood. And then, (if God bless and give success to your labours) I see not what hurt your Orchard can sustain.

CHAP. XV.

Of gathering and keeping Fruit.

General rule.

Although it be an easie matter, when God shall send it, to gather and keep fruit, yet are there certain things worthy your regard : You must gather your fruit when it is Ripe, and not before, else will it wither, and be tough and sowr. All fruits generally are Ripe, when they begin to fall : For trees do as all other bearers do, when their young ones are Ripe, they will wain them. The Dove her Pidgeons, the Coney her Rabbets, and Women their Children. Some fruit-trees sometimes getting a taint in the setting, with a Frost, or evil wind, will cast their fruit untimely, but not before they leave giving them sap, or they leave growing :

Cherries, &c.

Except from this aforesaid rule, Cherries, Damsons, and Bullis. The Cherry is Ripe when he is swelled, wholly Red, and sweet Damsons and Bullis not before the first frost.

Apples.

Apples are known to be ripe, partly by their colour, growing towards a yellow, except the Leather-coat, and some Pears, and Greenings.

When.

Timely Summer-fruit will be ready, some at Midsummer, most at Lammas for present use ; but generally, no keeping fruit before *Michaeltide*. Hard winter fruit, and Wardens longer.

Gather at the full of the Moon, for keeping, gather dry for fear of Rotting.

Dry stalks.

Gather the stalks withal, for a little wound in fruit

is deadly ; but not the stump, that must bear the next fruit ; nor leaves, for moisture putrifies.

Gather every kind severally by it self, for all will not keep alike, and it is hard to diicern them, when they are mingled. *Severally.*

If your trees be over-laden, (as they will be, being ordered, as is before taught) I like better of pulling some off, (though they be not ripe) near the top of the Bough, then of propping by much, the rest shall be better fed. Propping puts the boughs in danger, and frets it at least. *Over-laden trees.*

Instruments : A long Ladder of light Fir, a Stool ladder . . . A gathering-apron like a poak before you, made of purpose, or a Wallet hung on a bough, or a basket with a sieve bottom, or skin bottom, with lathes or splinters under, hung in a rope to pull up and down : bruise none, every bruise is to fruit death ; if you do, use them presently. An hook to pull boughs to you is necessary. Break no boughs. *Instruments.*

Bruises.

For keeping, lay them in a dry loft, the longest-keeping Apples first and furthest on dry straw, on heaps, ten or fourteen days, thick, that they may sweat. Then dry them with a soft and clean cloth, and lay them thin abroad. Long-keeping fruit would be turned once in a month softly ; but not in, nor immediately after frost. In a loft, cover'd well with straw, but rather with chaff or bran : For frost doth cause tender rottenness. *Keeping.*

CHAP. XVII.

Ornaments.

Methinks hitherto we have but a bare Orchard for fruit, and but half good, so long as it wants those comely Ornaments that should give beauty to all our labours, and make much for the honest delight of the owner and his friends.

<small>Delight the chief end of Orchards.</small>

For it is not to be doubted, but as God hath given man things profitable, so hath he allowed him honest comfort, delight, and recreation in all the works of his hands. Nay, all his labours under the Sun without this are troubles and vexations of mind : For what is greedy gain without delight, but moiling, and turmoiling in slavery? But comfortable delight, with content, is the good of every thing, and the pattern of Heaven. A morsel of bread with comfort, is better by much than a fat Ox with unquietness. And who can deny but the principal end of an Orchard, is the honest delight of one wearied with the work of his lawful calling? The very works of, and in an Orchard and Garden are better than the ease and rest of, and from other labours. When God had made a man after his own Images, in a perfect state, and would have him to represent himself in authority, tranquility, and pleasure upon the earth, he placed him in Paradise. What was Paradise? but a Garden, an Orchard of Trees and Herbs, full of pleasure, and nothing there but delights . . .

<small>Orchard delightsome.</small>

<small>An Orchard in Paradise.</small>

What can your eye desire to see, your ears to hear, your mouth to take, or your nose to smell, that is not to be had in an Orchard, with abundance of variety? What more delightsome than an infinite variety of sweet smelling flowers, decking with sundry colours, the green mantle of the earth, the universal mother of us all, so by them bespotted, so died, that all the World cannot sample them, and wherein it is more fit to admire the Dyer, than imitate his Workmanship, colouring not only the earth, but decking the air, and sweetning every breath and spirit.   *Causes of delight in any Orchard.*

The Rose red, Damask, Velvet, and double double Province-Rose, the sweet Musk-Rose double and single, the double and single white-Rose: The fair and sweet-senting Woodbine, double and single, and double double. Purple Cowslips, and double Cowslips, and double double Cowslips, Primrose double and single. The Violet nothing behind the best, for smelling sweetly. A thousand more will provoke your content.   *Flowers.*

And all these by the skill of your Gardiner, so comelily and orderly placed in your borders and squares, and so intermingled, that one looking thereon, cannot but wonder to see, what Nature, corrected by Art, can do.   *Borders and Squares.*

When you behold in divers corners of your Orchard *Mounts* of stone or wood, curiously wrought within and without, or of earth covered with Fruit-trees, Kentish Cherries, Damsons, Plums, *&c.* with stairs of precious workmanship; and in some corner (or more) a true Dial or Clock, and some Antick works; and especially silver-   *Mounts.*   *Dial.*

A. *All these squares must be set with Trees, the Garden and other Ornaments must stand in spaces betwixt the Trees, and in the borders and fences.*
B. *Trees twenty yards asunder.*
C. *Garden Knots.*

D. *Kitching Garden.*
E. *Bridge.*
F. *Conduit.*
G. *Stairs.*

H. *Walkes set with great wood thicke.*
I. *Walks set with great wood round about your Orchard.*
K. *The Out fence.*
L. *The Out fence set with stone-fruit.*

M. *Mount. To force Earth for a Mount or such like, set it round with quicke, and lay boughes of Trees strangely intermingled, the tops inward, with the Earth in the middle.*
N. *Still-house.*
O. *Good standing for Bees, if you have an house.*

P. *If the River run by your door, and under your Mount, it will be pleasant.*

sounding Musick, mixt Instruments, and Voices, gracing all the rest: How will you be wrapt with Delight?

    Large Walks, broad and long, close and open, like the *Tempe*-groves in *Thessaly*, raised with gravel and sand, having seats and banks of Camomile; all this delights the mind, and brings health to the body.

    View now with delight the works of your own hands, your Fruit-trees of all sorts, loaden with sweet blossoms, and fruit of all tastes, operations, and colours: your trees standing in comely order, which way soever you look.

    Your borders on every side hanging and dropping with Feberries, Raspberries, Barberries, Currans, and the Roots of your trees powdered with Strawberries, Red, White and Green, what a pleasure is this! Your Gardner can frame your lesser wood to the shape of men armed in the field, ready to give battle; of swift-running Grey-hounds, or of well-sented and true-running Hounds to chase the Deer, or hunt the Hare. This king of hunting shall not waste your Corn, nor much your Coyn

    Mazes well framed a man's height, may perhaps make your friend wander in gathering of Berries till he cannot recover himself without your help.

    To have occasion to exercise within your Orchard, it shall be a pleasure to have a bowling-Alley, or rather (which is more manly, and more healthful) a pair of Buts, to stretch your Arms.

    Rosemary and sweet Eglantine are seemly Ornaments about a Door or Window, and so is Woodbine.

Marginal notes: Musick. Walks. Seats. Order of trees. Shape of men and beasts. Mazes. Bowling-Alley. Buts. Herbs.

Look Chap. 15. and you shall see the form of a Conduit ; if there were two or more, it were not amiss.   *Conduit.*

And in mine own opinion, I could highly commend your Orchard, if either through it, or hard by it, there should run a pleasant River with silver streams, you might sit in your Mount, and angle a peckled Trout, sleighty Eel, or some other dainty Fish. Or Moats, whereon you may row with a Boat, and fish with Nets . . .   *River.* *Moats.*

A Vine overshadowing a seat, is very comely, though her Grapes with us ripen slowly.   *Vine.*

One chief grace that adorns an Orchard, I cannot let slip : a brood of Nightingales, who with several notes and tunes, with a strong delightsome voice out of a weak body, will bear you company night and day. She loves (and lives in) hots of woods in her heart. She will help you to cleanse your trees of Caterpillars, and all noy-some worms and flies. The gentle Robin-red-brest will help her, and in winter in the coldest storms will keep apart. Neither will the silly Wren be behind in Summer, with her distinct whistle, (like a sweet Recorder) to chear your spirits.   *Birds.* *Nightingale.* *Robin red-brest.* *Wren.*

The Black-bird and Throstle (for I take it, the Thrust sings not, but devours) sing loudly in a *May* morning, and delights the ear much, and you need not want their company, if you have ripe Cherries or Berries, and would as gladly as the rest do your pleasure : but I had rather want their company than my fruit.   *Black-bird.* *Thrush.*

What shall I say? A thousand of pleasant delights are attending an Orchard : and sooner shall I be weary, than I can reckon the least part of that pleasure, which one that hath, and loves an Orchard, may find therein.

What is there of all these few that I have reckoned, which do not pleasure the eye, the ear, the smell and taste? And by the senses, as Organs, Pipes and Windows, these delights are carried to refresh the gentle, generous and noble mind.

To conclude, What joy may you have, that you living to such an age, shall see the blessing of God on your labours while you live, and leave behind you to heirs of successors, (for God will make heirs) such a work, that many ages after your death shall record your love to their Country? And the rather, when you consider to what length of time your work is to last.

Your own labour.

FINIS.